D1538914

My United States
South Dakota

JO S. KITTINGER

Children's Press®
An Imprint of Scholastic Inc.

Content Consultant

James Wolfinger, PhD, Associate Dean and Professor
College of Education, DePaul University, Chicago, Illinois

Library of Congress Cataloging-in-Publication Data
Names: Kittinger, Jo S., author.
Title: South Dakota / by Jo S. Kittinger.
Description: New York, NY : Scholastic Inc., [2019] | Series: A true book | Includes bibliographical references and index.
Identifiers: LCCN 2017054607 | ISBN 9780531235805 (library binding) | ISBN 9780531250938 (pbk.)
Subjects: LCSH: South Dakota—Juvenile literature.
Classification: LCC F651.3 .K57 2019 | DDC 978.3—dc23
LC record available at https://lccn.loc.gov/2017054607

All rights reserved. Published in 2018 by Children's Press, an imprint of Scholastic Inc.
Printed in North Mankato, MN, USA 113

SCHOLASTIC, CHILDREN'S PRESS, A TRUE BOOK™, and associated logos are trademarks and/or registered trademarks of Scholastic Inc.

Scholastic Inc., 557 Broadway, New York, NY 10012

1 2 3 4 5 6 7 8 9 10 R 28 27 26 25 24 23 22 21 20 19

Front cover: A park worker examines cracks in Mount Rushmore

Back cover: Badlands National Park

Welcome to South Dakota

Find the Truth!

Key Facts

Capital: Pierre

Estimated population as of 2017: 865,454

Nickname: Mount Rushmore State

Biggest cities: Sioux Falls, Rapid City, Aberdeen

UNITED STATES

South Dakota

Everything you are about to read is true *except* for one of the sentences on this page.

Which one is **TRUE**?

T or F Black-footed ferrets are extremely common in South Dakota.

T or F South Dakota has one of the lowest unemployment rates in the country.

1AE F27

GREAT FACES. GREAT PLACES.

Find the answers in this book.

Contents

THE BIG TRUTH!

American
pasque

What Represents South Dakota?

Triceratops fossil

Barrel racing

3 History

How did South Dakota become
the state it is today?

4 Culture

What do South Dakotans do for work and fun?

Crazy Horse
Memorial

This Is South Dakota!

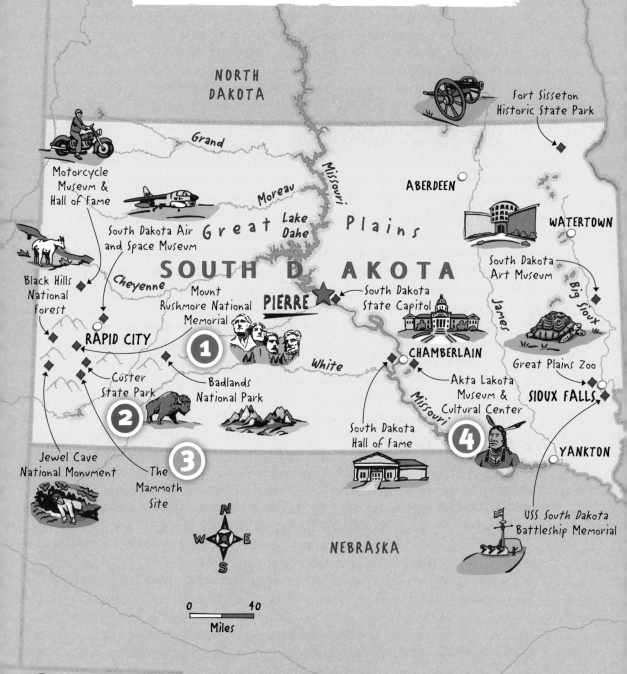

NORTH DAKOTA

Grand

Moreau

Missouri

Lake Dahe

Cheyenne

Great Plains

SOUTH D AKOTA

ABERDEEN

WATERTOWN

Fort Sisseton Historic State Park

Motorcycle Museum & Hall of fame

South Dakota Air and Space Museum

Black Hills National Forest

Mount Rushmore National Memorial

PIERRE

South Dakota State Capitol

South Dakota Art Museum

Big Sioux

James

RAPID CITY

(1)

White

CHAMBERLAIN

Great Plains Zoo

SIOUX FALLS

Custer State Park

Badlands National Park

(2)

Akta Lakota Museum & Cultural Center

South Dakota Hall of fame

Missouri

(4)

YANKTON

Jewel Cave National Monument

(3)

The Mammoth Site

USS South Dakota Battleship Memorial

NEBRASKA

N
W E
S

0   40
Miles

① Mount Rushmore National Memorial

Sculptor Gutzon Borglum carved U.S. presidents George Washington, Thomas Jefferson, Theodore Roosevelt, and Abraham Lincoln into this granite mountain in southwestern South Dakota.

② Custer State Park

This park in the southwestern part of the state offers amazing scenery and plentiful wildlife, including bison, elk, pronghorn, deer, prairie dogs, wild burros, and more.

③ The Mammoth Site

In Hot Springs, visitors can tour this active dig site where many mammoth skeletons have been uncovered. Fossils of other Ice Age animals discovered here include llamas and giant bears.

④ Akta Lakota Museum and Cultural Center

This museum in Chamberlain celebrates the Native American way of life, past and present. Art, artifacts, and displays show the history and culture of the Lakota Sioux.

Badlands National Park covers 244,000 acres (98,743 hectares) of South Dakota.

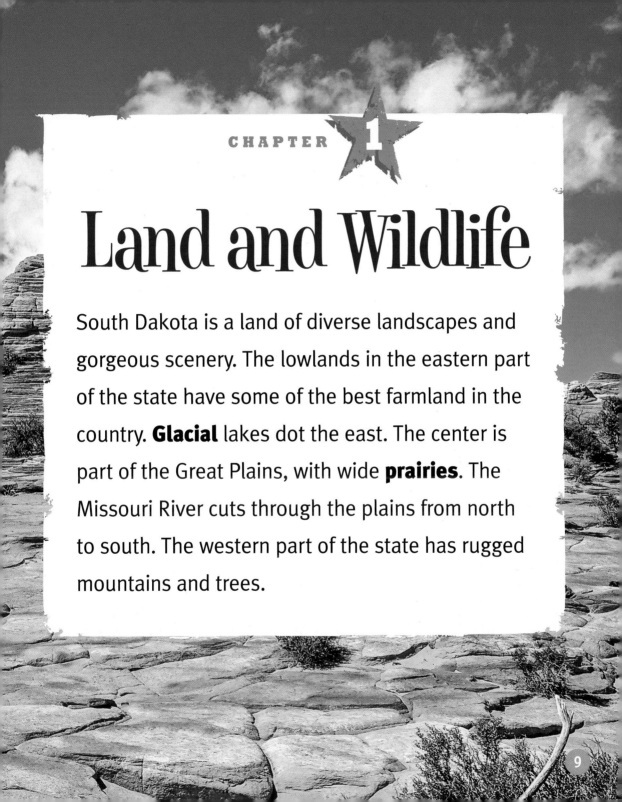

CHAPTER 1

Land and Wildlife

South Dakota is a land of diverse landscapes and gorgeous scenery. The lowlands in the eastern part of the state have some of the best farmland in the country. **Glacial** lakes dot the east. The center is part of the Great Plains, with wide **prairies**. The Missouri River cuts through the plains from north to south. The western part of the state has rugged mountains and trees.

The Lay of the Land

South Dakota is in the north-central United States. It is bordered by North Dakota, Minnesota, Iowa, Nebraska, Wyoming, and Montana. South Dakota is a midsize state, but it has one of the smallest populations in the country, ranking 46th out of all the states. As a result, it is also one of the most sparsely populated states, with few major cities and large areas of land where no one lives.

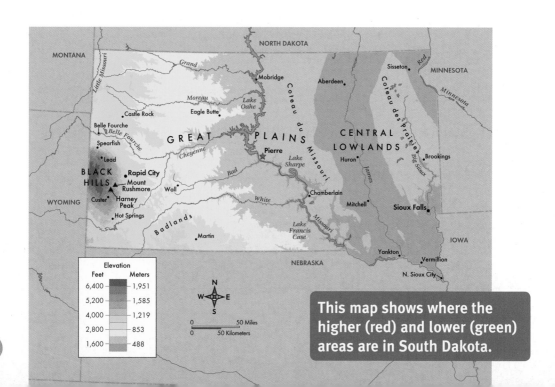

This map shows where the higher (red) and lower (green) areas are in South Dakota.

Jewel Cave

South Dakota has several impressive caves. Jewel Cave, in Black Hills National Forest, is the third-longest cave in the world. It has over 180 miles (290 kilometers) of mapped passages. The cave's chambers are filled with crystals, stalagmites, stalactites, and other formations. Visitors can see gypsum deposits in the shapes of needles, beards, flowers, and spiders. The cave stays a chilly 49 degrees Fahrenheit (9 degrees Celsius) year-round.

There are several large "rooms" within Jewel Cave, each with its own collection of fascinating rock formations.

On June 24, 2003, a record-setting 67 tornadoes touched down in South Dakota within a span of 8 hours.

From Season to Season

South Dakota has four distinct seasons, and residents often face extreme temperatures. Heat can soar above 100°F (38°C) in July and August. Temperatures regularly dip below freezing in winter. Blizzards bring heavy snowfall and gusting wind. In spring and autumn, the temperatures can change drastically in a day. All year long, the state is windy. Severe thunderstorms, especially in summer months, can produce hail or tornadoes.

Prairies, Farms, and Forests

The Great Plains were once a great sea of grass. Much of the native prairie has been lost to farming, but there are still some pockets remaining. Some prairies have tall grasses, some have short grasses, and some are mixed. Wildflowers bloom among the grasses.

Most of South Dakota's trees are found in the Black Hills area. There, forests of pine trees and Black Hills spruce are common.

South Dakota is one of the top states for sunflowers. Many grow on farms, while others spring up in the wild.

Park biologists in Wind Cave National Park and in the Badlands are working to save black-footed ferrets from extinction.

All Kinds of Animals

From tiny shrews to huge bison, a wide variety of mammals live in South Dakota. Other large species include deer, elk, pronghorn, and bighorn sheep. Wild horses live in a Black Hills sanctuary. Prairie dogs dig "towns" of underground chambers connected by tunnels. Badgers, bobcats, coyotes, and foxes are often seen around these towns, looking to make meals of the prairie dogs. Beavers, minks, and muskrats can be found near water. Black-footed ferrets are an endangered species found in the state.

South Dakota's rivers and lakes support many species of fish. There are walleyes, bass, catfish, perch, and more. Over 400 species of birds have been seen in the state, from tiny hummingbirds to majestic bald eagles. South Dakota's wetlands provide homes for ducks, geese, and shorebirds. Songbirds flock to forests, while hawks and owls hunt across the state. Many kinds of reptiles and amphibians can also be found in South Dakota.

The prairie rattlesnake is the only venomous snake in the state.

South Dakota's capitol is 161 feet (49 meters) tall, 190 feet (58 m) wide, and 292 feet (89 m) long.

CHAPTER 2

Government

When South Dakota became a state in 1889, Pierre was chosen as the temporary capital. The following year, it was named the permanent capital. On three occasions in the following years, residents voted on whether to move the capital elsewhere. Each time, Pierre remained South Dakota's capital city. The grand capitol was constructed partly to stop any more talk of moving the capital from Pierre. Construction on the building began in 1905 and was completed in 1910.

Three Branches

South Dakota, like other states, has three branches of government. The legislative branch consists of the Senate and the House of Representatives. It writes laws. The executive branch, headed by the governor, carries out these laws. The judicial branch, made up of the state's courts, interprets laws. In addition, there are nine tribal governments that oversee Native American laws in the state.

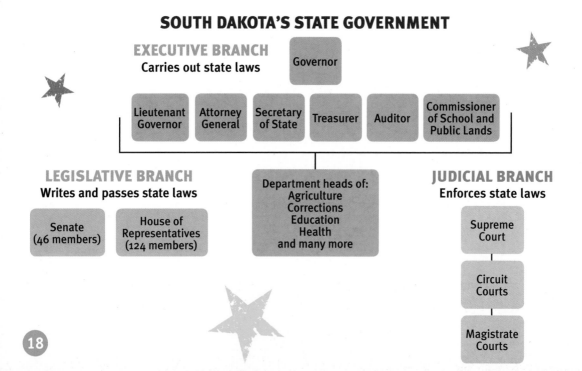

SOUTH DAKOTA'S STATE GOVERNMENT

EXECUTIVE BRANCH
Carries out state laws

Governor

| Lieutenant Governor | Attorney General | Secretary of State | Treasurer | Auditor | Commissioner of School and Public Lands |

LEGISLATIVE BRANCH
Writes and passes state laws

Senate (46 members)

House of Representatives (124 members)

Department heads of:
Agriculture
Corrections
Education
Health
and many more

JUDICIAL BRANCH
Enforces state laws

Supreme Court

Circuit Courts

Magistrate Courts

South Dakota's local governments each oversee their own police force.

Government by the People

Elected officials make decisions that affect the whole state. Voting for these officials gives citizens a voice in their government. South Dakotans can also propose laws on their own. Sometimes, people must go further to make their feelings known. Citizens can sign petitions to force the legislative branch to pay attention to their ideas. Participating in local government, at the town or county level, is another way South Dakotans can get involved.

South Dakota's National Role

Each state elects officials to represent it in the U.S. Congress. Like every state, South Dakota has two senators. The U.S. House of Representatives relies on a state's population to determine its numbers. South Dakota has one representative in the House.

Every four years, states vote on the next U.S. president. Each state is granted a number of electoral votes based on its number of members in Congress. With two senators and one representative, South Dakota has three electoral votes.

2 senators and 1 representative

3 electoral votes

With three electoral votes, South Dakota's voice in presidential elections is below average compared to other states.

The People of South Dakota

Elected officials in South Dakota represent a population with a range of interests, lifestyles, and backgrounds.

Ethnicity (2016 estimates)

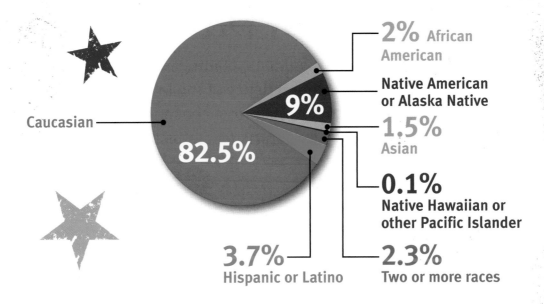

2% African American

Native American or Alaska Native **9%**

1.5% Asian

0.1% Native Hawaiian or other Pacific Islander

2.3% Two or more races

3.7% Hispanic or Latino

Caucasian **82.5%**

3% of South Dakotans were born in other countries.

24.6% are under the age of 18.

50.4% are male, and **49.6%** are female.

91.2% of adults graduated from high school.

67.8% own their homes.

27.5% of adults have a degree beyond high school.

6.5% speak a language other than English at home.

What Represents South Dakota?

States choose specific animals, plants, and objects to represent the values and characteristics of the land and its people. Find out why these symbols were chosen to represent South Dakota or discover surprising curiosities about them.

Seal

The basic design of South Dakota's state seal was created by Dr. Joseph Ward, the founder of Yankton College. It was adopted in 1885, four years before South Dakota became a state. The wording was changed from "State of Dakota" to "State of South Dakota" in 1889, when statehood was granted. The importance of mining, agriculture, and transportation on the Missouri River can be seen in the design.

Flag

The current flag was adopted in 1992 when South Dakota's official nickname changed from "the Sunshine State" to "the Mount Rushmore State." However, the flag continues to feature a blazing sun on a sky-blue field, with the state seal overlaying the sun.

American Pasque

STATE FLOWER

This beautiful purple flower grows wild in South Dakota's prairies.

Honeybee

STATE INSECT

South Dakota is a leader in honey production, and bees are important pollinators of crops.

Coyote

STATE ANIMAL

Coyotes appear often in Native American tales, usually as very clever tricksters.

Ring-Necked Pheasant

STATE BIRD

Native to Asia, the ring-necked pheasant was introduced to South Dakota in 1908.

Triceratops

STATE FOSSIL

A *Triceratops* skull discovered in Harding County in 1927 is on display in Rapid City.

Walleye

STATE FISH

Walleyes are popular with fishers because they are a challenge to catch and delicious to eat.

About 10,000 people flooded into the Black Hills during the gold rush of the 1870s.

A train passes through the Black Hills in the late 1800s.

CHAPTER 3

History

In 1874, the Dakotas were not yet states. There had long been rumors of gold in the Black Hills. According to the **Treaty** of Laramie, that area belonged to the Sioux. The U.S. Army sent over 1,000 men, led by Lieutenant Colonel George Custer, to find out if the gold rumor was true. It was. Thousands of gold seekers soon flooded the Sioux's territory, and the Black Hills would never be the same.

Native Americans

People first arrived in what is now South Dakota by about 13,000 to 14,000 years ago. Later, the Arikara people settled in the area. They built villages with homes made from earth and established a trade network with other tribes. By the early 1700s, **nomadic** Sioux tribes dominated the area. The Sioux hunted bison, deer, and other animals. They ate the animals' meat and turned their hides and bones into useful items such as clothing and tools.

This map shows some of the major tribes that lived in what is now South Dakota before Europeans came.

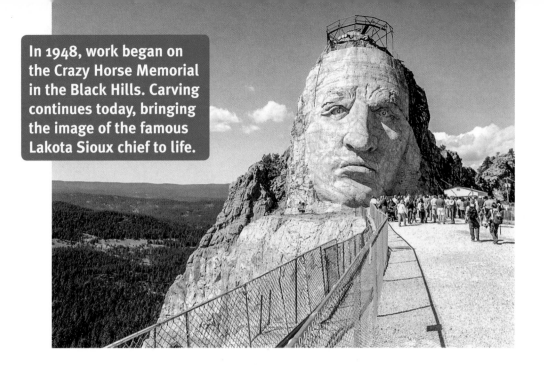

In 1948, work began on the Crazy Horse Memorial in the Black Hills. Carving continues today, bringing the image of the famous Lakota Sioux chief to life.

White people first came to South Dakota in the 1700s. As white settlers moved into the area, treaties were made and broken with Native Americans. Tribes were settled into certain areas and then forced off those lands.

Today, South Dakota has nine tribal governments with designated lands. Each is unique, but most are part of the Sioux Nation. Native Americans in South Dakota continue to seek equal rights and better standards of living.

Early Exploration

The first white people to enter present-day South Dakota were the La Vérendrye brothers in 1743. These explorers claimed the region for France. In 1803, the United States purchased the Louisiana Territory from France. It included the region that is now South Dakota. The next year, President Thomas Jefferson sent Meriwether Lewis and William Clark to explore the area. They traveled the Missouri River, made maps, and noted the plants and animals they saw.

This map shows routes Europeans took as they explored and settled what is now South Dakota.

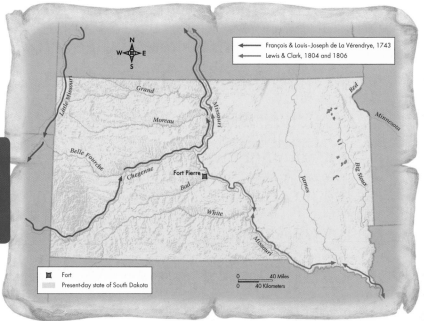

François & Louis–Joseph de La Vérendrye, 1743
Lewis & Clark, 1804 and 1806

Little Missouri
Grand
Moreau
Belle Fourche
Cheyenne
Fort Pierre
Bad
White
Missouri
James
Red
Minnesota
Big Sioux

Fort
Present-day state of South Dakota

0   40 Miles
0   40 Kilometers

The reports created by Lewis and Clark led to the building of trading posts and forts in the region. Fur trading was big business. In 1817, the area's first permanent settlement was built at Fort Pierre. The fort received goods shipped from St. Louis, Missouri. Coffee, tobacco, beans, tin cups, knives, and fabric were traded with Native Americans for buffalo hides. Unfortunately, diseases such as smallpox also spread from the white settlers to the Native Americans. This resulted in many deaths.

Road to Statehood

Population in the western part of the Dakota Territory exploded with the gold rush of the late 1800s. Railroad lines soon reached the Black Hills, and there began to be talk of statehood. Some residents wanted a single state of Dakota, while others wanted two states. The two-state option won. In 1889, North and South Dakota were admitted into the United States at the same time.

Timeline of South Dakota Events

11,000 BCE
People have arrived in what is now South Dakota by this time.

1743
The La Vérendrye brothers bury a lead plate near the site of Fort Pierre, claiming the land for France.

| 11,000 BCE | 1700–1750 CE | 1743 | 1804 |

1700–1750 CE
The Sioux Nation gains control of the northern Plains after battles with the Arikara, Mandan, and Omaha.

1804
Lewis and Clark explore the Missouri River

Even after statehood, there continued to be conflicts over land in South Dakota. In 1890, the Wounded Knee **Massacre** happened on the Pine Ridge Indian Reservation. This was the last major battle between the Sioux and the U.S. government. After the defeat of the Sioux, railroad companies sold land to farmers and built small towns. Settlers flowed into the state. They built houses of **sod** and planted crops such as corn and wheat. Ranchers raised cattle.

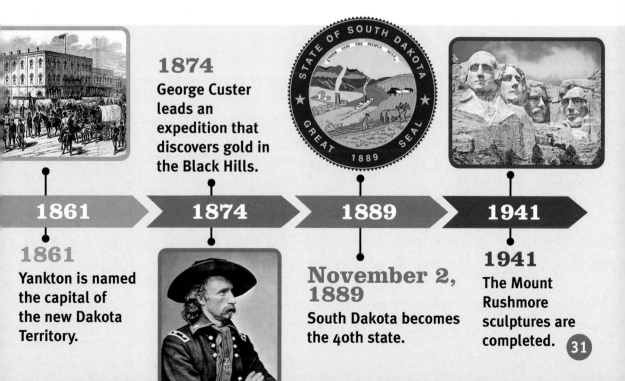

1874
George Custer leads an expedition that discovers gold in the Black Hills.

1861 → **1874** → **1889** → **1941**

1861
Yankton is named the capital of the new Dakota Territory.

November 2, 1889
South Dakota becomes the 40th state.

1941
The Mount Rushmore sculptures are completed.

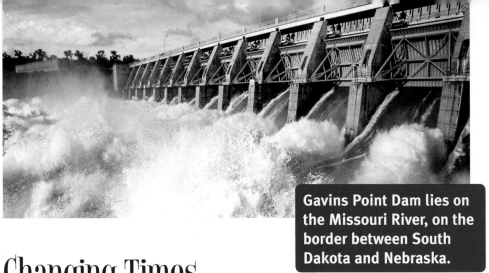

Gavins Point Dam lies on the Missouri River, on the border between South Dakota and Nebraska.

Changing Times

The 20th century saw several major events in South Dakota history. During World War II (1939–1945), Sioux soldiers sent and received messages in codes spoken in their native languages. Many of these "code talkers" came from South Dakota. In 1944, the Flood Control Act led to the building of several dams on the Missouri River. The dams provided jobs, generated electricity, controlled flooding, and created lakes for recreation.

Today, South Dakota provides crops and livestock to the country. Tourists enjoy the state's spectacular parks and monuments.

A Monumental Man

Gutzon Borglum was asked to create a sculpture to bring tourists to South Dakota. Borglum dreamed big. He chose Mount Rushmore in western South Dakota as the site and planned to carve the heads of four presidents into the mountain. Work began in 1927.

Most of the carving was done with dynamite. About 400 men worked on the sculpture with ropes, pulleys, ladders, and **scaffolds**. Borglum spent the rest of his life on the project. He died in 1941. Shortly after his death, Congress declared the monument finished.

Borglum's original design included more than just the presidents' heads.

CHAPTER 4

Culture

The arts are alive in South Dakota. In Sioux Falls, the Washington Pavilion hosts art exhibits, concerts, and dance productions. In the summer, plays are performed at the Black Hills Playhouse. The South Dakota Symphony Orchestra provides high-quality performances. At the state's powwows, Native Americans in colorful traditional costumes dance, sing, and play drums.

The Cheyenne River Sioux Tribe Powwow, Fair, and Rodeo is held each year in north-central South Dakota.

South Dakotans at Play

Winter fun in South Dakota includes skiing, snowboarding, snowshoeing, and ice fishing. Summer is perfect for hiking, camping, or golf. Fans follow college and minor league basketball, baseball, and hockey. But rodeo is the biggest sport in South Dakota. Rodeo is rooted in the state's cowboy history. Kids start young with mutton busting (sheep riding) and barrel racing (steering horses around barrels). They then move up to **roughstock** training.

The Black Hills Roundup rodeo has been held each year since 1918.

The Sturgis Motorcycle Rally offers races, musical performances, and even a beard-growing contest.

Statewide Celebrations

South Dakotans enjoy two major fairs each year—the Sioux Empire Fair and the State Fair. There are rides, agricultural exhibits, concerts, and more. In Tabor, Czech Days attracts large crowds for traditional food and dancing. Schmeckfest, in Freeman, celebrates German culture and features a musical play. Life on the prairie is re-created at the Laura Ingalls Wilder Pageant, in De Smet. The state's biggest annual event is the Sturgis Motorcycle Rally, which draws over 500,000 riders!

South Dakota at Work

The economy in South Dakota has been quietly booming in recent years. Agriculture remains the top industry. There are more cows than people in the state! Farmers plant corn, wheat, and soybeans. Factories build computer parts

There are nearly five cows for every person in South Dakota.

and process food. Materials such as granite, limestone, and gravel are mined. Tourism and casinos are major industries. With so many jobs available, South Dakota has one of the lowest unemployment rates in the country.

Tourism in the Black Hills

During the gold rush, jobs in the Black Hills focused on miners and their needs. Jobs in the area now focus on meeting the needs of visitors. Many locals work at restaurants, hotels, and stores. Memorials, parks, and caves hire people to handle the crowds. Casino jobs include dealers and security officers. Deadwood, no longer the lawless mining town it used to be, entertains tourists with pretend gunfights during the annual Wild Bill Days event. All this activity flourishes amid the natural beauty of the Black Hills.

Many of the buildings in Deadwood have been designed to preserve the town's Old West flavor.

What's for Dinner?

South Dakota meals blend the cultures of Native Americans and European settlers. German, Scandinavian, and Native American dishes might be served side by side. Chislic is a favorite dish. It is made from cubes of meat—usually beef, lamb, or venison—fried on **skewers**. Many South Dakotans love tacos served on Native American fry bread.

 ## South Dakota Tacos

 Ask an adult to help you!

This delicious taco recipe uses fry bread, a tasty flatbread invented by Native Americans.

Ingredients
1 pound ground beef
1 package taco seasoning
8 fry breads
Toppings: chopped lettuce, chopped tomatoes, grated cheddar cheese, sour cream, salsa

Directions
Cook the ground beef with the taco seasoning as directed on the package. Place a scoop of meat on each fry bread and add the toppings. Enjoy!

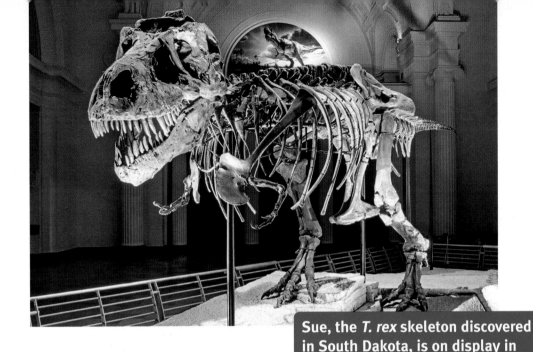

Sue, the *T. rex* skeleton discovered in South Dakota, is on display in Chicago's Field Museum.

A Stupendous State

South Dakota is perhaps most famous for the towering sculptures on Mount Rushmore. But not all of the state's amazing features rise so high above the ground. Some of the interesting things are actually located beneath the surface! The largest, most complete *Tyrannosaurus rex* skeleton ever found was dug up in South Dakota in 1990. Rich history, fruitful land, and stunning natural beauty— these are at the heart of South Dakota! ★

Famous People

York

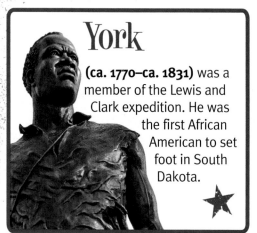

(ca. 1770–ca. 1831) was a member of the Lewis and Clark expedition. He was the first African American to set foot in South Dakota.

Sitting Bull

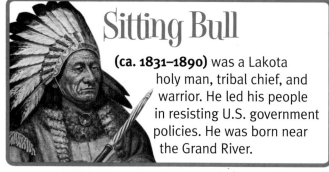

(ca. 1831–1890) was a Lakota holy man, tribal chief, and warrior. He led his people in resisting U.S. government policies. He was born near the Grand River.

Oscar Micheaux

(1884–1951) settled in South Dakota in the early 1900s and wrote several books about his life there. In 1919, he turned one of them into a film called *The Homesteader*. It was the first full-length film made by an African American.

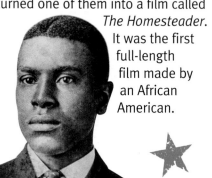

Laura Ingalls Wilder

(1867–1957) is the author of the beloved Little House on the Prairie books. She lived with her family in De Smet.

Ernest Lawrence

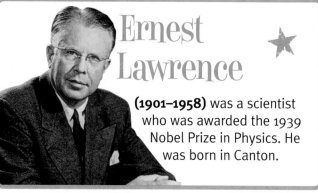

(1901–1958) was a scientist who was awarded the 1939 Nobel Prize in Physics. He was born in Canton.

Hubert Humphrey

(1911–1978) served as vice president of the United States from 1965 to 1969 and ran for president in 1968. He was born in Wallace.

George McGovern

(1922–2012) was a politician who served as both a U.S. representative and a senator and ran for president in 1972. He was born in Avon and grew up in Mitchell.

Billy Mills

(1938–), a gifted runner, won an Olympic gold medal in the 10,000-meter (6.2-mile) race in 1964. He was born in Pine Ridge, and his Oglala name is Makata Taka Hela.

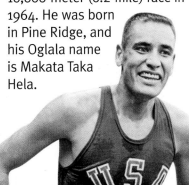

Bob Barker

(1923–) is the former host of *The Price Is Right* game show. He had a 50-year career in TV and won 19 Emmy Awards. He spent much of his youth on the Rosebud Indian Reservation.

George "Sparky" Anderson

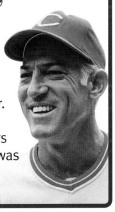

(1934–2010) was a Major League Baseball player, coach, and manager. He led the Cincinnati Reds to two championships and the Detroit Tigers to another. Born in Bridgewater, he was elected to the Baseball Hall of Fame in 2000.

Brock Lesnar

(1977–) is the longest-running WWE wrestling Universal Champion. He is also an NCAA wrestling champion and mixed martial arts champion. He was born in Webster.

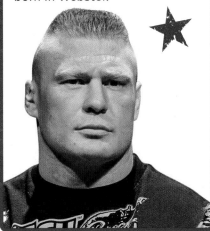

Did You Know That ...

The Great Plains are not all prairie. There are also dramatic rock formations and canyons in the area.

A huge herd of wild bison is rounded up each year in Custer State Park. The animals are then led into corrals, where park workers can inspect them and make sure the herd is healthy. Huge crowds come from all around to witness this event.

Fossils of many extinct animals, such as this saber-toothed tiger, have been found in Badlands National Park in southwestern South Dakota.

MITCHELL CORN PALACE

The word *Dakota* means "friend" or "ally" in the Sioux language.

The Corn Palace in Mitchell is covered in pictures created from corn, grain, and grasses.

The Crazy Horse Memorial was started in 1948 and is still far from being finished.

Did you find the truth?

(F) Black-footed ferrets are extremely common in South Dakota.

(T) South Dakota has one of the lowest unemployment rates in the country.

Resources

Books

Burgan, Michael. *South Dakota*. New York: Scholastic, 2015.

Coury, Tina Nichols. *Hanging Off Jefferson's Nose: Growing Up on Mount Rushmore*. New York: Dial Books for Young Readers, 2012.

Meinking, Mary. *What's Great About South Dakota?* Minneapolis: Lerner Publishing Group, 2015.

Patrick, Jean L. S. *Who Carved the Mountain? The Story of Mount Rushmore*. Rapid City, SD: Mount Rushmore History Association, 2005.

Rozett, Louise (ed.). *Fast Facts About the 50 States: Plus Puerto Rico and Washington, D.C.* New York: Children's Press, 2010.

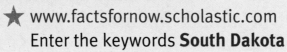

Visit this Scholastic website for more information on South Dakota:
★ www.factsfornow.scholastic.com
Enter the keywords **South Dakota**

Important Words

glacial (GLAY-shuhl) created by the melting of a glacier, a slow-moving mass of ice found in mountain valleys or polar regions

massacre (MASS-uh-kur) the violent killing of a large number of people at the same time, often in battle

nomadic (noh-MAD-ik) describing members of a community that travels from place to place instead of living in the same place all the time

prairies (PRAIR-eez) large areas of flat or rolling grassland with few or no trees

roughstock (RUFF-stahk) a category of events in rodeo, including bull riding, saddle bronco riding, calf roping, and steer wrestling

scaffolds (SKAF-uhldz) temporary, raised structures made of planks and poles that serve as platforms for workers doing construction

skewers (SKYOO-urz) long metal or wooden pins for holding pieces of meat or vegetables together while they are being cooked

sod (SAHD) the top layer of soil with the grass that grows in it

treaty (TREE-tee) a formal written agreement between two or more countries

Index

Page numbers in **bold** indicate illustrations.

About the Author

Jo S. Kittinger loves traveling and adventure. She enjoys exploring national parks around the country. Jo is the author of over 25 books for children. You might find her kayaking or taking photographs of animals or wildflowers.